TIN'
FOR KIDS

BY

Inventing new kinds of play

ILLUSTRATED BY
SAVANNA GANUCHEAU

COVER ILLUSTRATION BY
PAULINA GANUCHEAU

HELLO!

THESE GAMES ARE DESIGNED FOR ONE GROWNUP TO PLAY WITH A BUNCH OF KIDS!

Beside the title of each game is a listing of how many kids can play. Most of the games can be played with more grown-ups, but if you ever need more than one grownup, the game will specify this.

We've split the book into two sections: games for indoors and games for outdoors. Don't worry if you've got a favourite game and want to play it everywhere. Most of these games will work in any context with a little imagination. These games are safe, but use common sense! Silliness is encouraged, but foolishness is not.

This book is not designed to be read in order. Why don't you pick a random page and get playing? Or head to the list at the back of the book to find a game with the most fun-sounding name!

TINY CONTENTS

INTRODUCTION

Ten years ago, a new addition was announced for the National Toy Hall Of Fame in New York: the cardboard box. In among the videogame consoles and Barbies and yo-yos that made up the rest of the list, it looked out of place. A cardboard box wasn't designed as a toy, or meant for children, or even for fun. A cardboard box is a boring, brown lump, something that only matters because of what might be in it, not because of what it is.

But every child, and every grown-up child, can tell you the opposite. The cardboard box deserves to be on that list, maybe even more than some of the bright, brash toys that are forgotten within a generation. It deserves its place because the cardboard box knows a secret about toys. A cardboard box knows that toys don't exist.

There's no such thing as a toy. A toy is name we give to any object that helps us play. Sometimes that object is a doll, or a ball, or a puzzle. Sometimes it's a Playstation, or a water pistol, or ten thousand pieces of Lego. But sometimes it's a cardboard box, or a blanket, or a park bench or a crack in the pavement.

Tiny Games For Kids knows the same secret that cardboard boxes know – everything has some playfulness hidden inside it if you just know the right way to look at it. Making this book gave us a chance to discover hundreds of new toys. We hope that spending a little time with it will fill your world with toys you never knew you had.

    – Margaret Robertson

GAMES FOR INDOORS

POSTURE PERFECT

2+

ARE THERE ANY MAGAZINES AROUND?

In this game players balance magazines on their head for as long as they can.

First, have the kids stand in front of you. Have them practice standing very straight, and very still. Now place a magazine on their head. For an easier challenge, use an open magazine, or for a tougher challenge, keep it closed. Once it's balanced on there, point to something across the room and see if they can walk to it without losing the magazine. And no using their hands!

Challenge mode: have the players keep the magazine on their head while you tell jokes, or even tickle!

NO-LOOK HIGH FIVE

1

CLOSED EYE, FIVE HIGH

You'll need to sit across from each other, and high five. Then do it again, but very softly. Then both grownup and kid will close their eyes and try to high five! If you've mastered the high-five, try to touch each other's noses with your thumbs instead, while your eyes are closed! It's harder than it sounds, isn't it?

CAT CATCH

2+

DO YOU HAVE A TABLE KIDS CAN GET UNDER, AND SOME SMALL OBJECTS THEY CAN COLLECT, LIKE STUFFED ANIMALS OR BLOCKS?

In this game kids pretend to be busy cats, while the grownup is a dog who tries to tag them.

Scatter some toys or small objects around the room (if the kids have not already done so). These are your mice! Have all the kids get under the table. Explain that they are a team of cats who are 'safe' here and you cannot touch them. However, when they are out from under the table, you will try and tag them. If you do, they have to sit out for the rest of the game (or a short time, if that will work better for your group).

The kids' goal is to collect all the mice scattered around the room, without you catching them. If the kids can collect all the mice and bring them back to under the table, they win! If you tag all the kids first, play again! Okay ready? GO!

STUFFED ANIMAL AIRLINES

2+

DO YOU HAVE A TOWEL, A SOFA, AND A STUFFED ANIMAL? AND ARE YOU COOL WITH STUFFED ANIMALS FLYING AROUND THE ROOM?

This is a game where everyone tries to launch a stuffed animal onto the couch using a towel.

Gather the kids together several feet from the couch and give them a towel and the stuffed animal (try to find one that's not afraid of flying). Help the kids hold the towel so that it's stretched tight between the group. Place the stuffed animal onto the stretched towel. Tell everyone that it wants to fly to the couch, but it can't afford first class. On the count of three, everyone has to use the towel to launch the stuffed animal onto the couch. Count to three and LAUNCH! You all win if the stuffed animal makes it. How was the flight?

Challenge mode: take a step back after each successful landing. Can you make it to three steps back?

CUP HANDED ROBOTS

DO YOU HAVE SEVERAL PLASTIC CUPS?

This is a race to see how fast you can pick things up with cups on your hands.

Scatter several soft objects (clothes, stuffed animals, towels) around the room. When you're done, have everyone put their hands in plastic cups. When you say 'GO!' everyone races to pick up things and put them in a basket (or pile) at your feet. How quickly did the robots collect everything? Once everything is picked up, count out the objects in the pile to see how many points the team scored.

Tip: you can use this game to get kids to clean their room. Cleaning is always better with robots.

THAT'S NOT HOW IT GOES! 1-3

DO YOU HAVE ACCESS TO A FAVOURITE BOOK, OR CAN YOU REMEMBER A FAVOURITE STORY?

In this game, the grownup tries to trick the other players by changing some of the key words in a favourite book or story.

Choose a book that the kids know well, or a story from memory. Start the story, but occasionally change a few of the key words, phrases, names, or details. Listeners get a point for each change they catch. You get a point for each change they don't. How did your story turn out?

DON'T FALL OFF THE BRIDGE!

1+

CAN YOU GET YOUR HANDS ON SOME MASKING TAPE OR BLUE PAINTERS TAPE?

In this game players try to cross the Tickle Bridge without falling off!

Starting by using tape to make a long line on the floor. Tell everyone that this is the Tickle Bridge. The kids have to cross it, but if they fall off, they will be tickled by the trolls who live under the bridge! Pick someone to cross the bridge first. Everyone else acts as the tickle trolls. If the person crossing the bridge steps off the tape, the tickle trolls can gently tickle them. Keep playing until everyone has crossed the bridge (or given up).

Challenge mode: put some twists and turns into the tape path!

RAIN OR SHINE?

1-3

CAN YOU GET ACCESS TO A SMARTPHONE, OR A COMPUTER?

This is a game about guessing what the weather is like – in places you aren't!

First, tell the kids that this is a game about imagining what the weather is like somewhere far away. Start by picking a place that's local to you and the kids, a neighbouring town or city should work.

Ask the kids if they think that place is sunny or not sunny today. Rain, snow, and cloudy all count as 'not sunny'. Once the kids have guessed, look up the weather. If the kids guessed right, give high fives and play with a new (farther away) city. If the kids guess right three times in a row, they win!

Challenge mode: give the kids some weather choices they can guess between like sunny, rainy, cloudy, or snowy.

Super challenge mode: guess temperatures!

WHAT'S MISSING?!? 1+

ARE THERE FIVE TO TEN DIFFERENT SMALL OBJECTS AROUND THAT YOU CAN SPREAD OUT ON A TABLE?

In this game, players have to remember what was there before, but now is gone.

Arrange a bunch of objects on a table and point out each one to the group. Say each thing out loud together. Now all the kids close their eyes, and you remove ONE of the things. Hide it out of sight! Everyone opens their eyes. Who can guess what's missing? Whoever guessed right gets to remove the next object. To make the game harder, start with more objects.

Ultimate tricky mode: add objects while people have their eyes closed. How many objects can you handle before it's too tricky?

HAT TOWERS

1-3

DO YOU HAVE SOME HATS?
ACTUALLY, A LOT OF HATS?

In this game the grownup tries to make the tallest tower they can – on the kids' heads!

Lay out a bunch of hats. Go for variety and quantity. Players should be standing VERY still. Put as many hats as you can on the first player. Count each one out loud. Keep going until the hats fall off. Now put as many hats as you can on the next player. Whoever wears the most hats, wins!

Bonus round: players have to walk around the room without spilling their hat towers!

LINE ARTISTS

1-2

DO YOU HAVE SOMETHING TO WRITE WITH
AND SOME PAPER YOU CAN DRAW ON?

Start by drawing a single line (curved or straight) anywhere on the paper. Now it's the next player's turn. Have them draw a new line somewhere. It can be connected to yours, or separate.

Take turns drawing lines until you've finished your masterpiece! Sign your names and donate it to a museum, or hang it on the refrigerator. Want a more structured challenge? Name an object before you start and work together to draw it, line by line.

KID RULERS

1+

KIDS ARE SURPRISINGLY USEFUL.

Ask everyone to guess how far it is from one side of the room to the other, measured in kids. Is it one kid long? Two kids long? Fifty kids long?!?

Now measure! Have a kid lay down with their feet against one wall. Lie the next kid down with their feet on the first kid's shoulders… Continue measuring with kids. When you run out, have the first kid get up and lie with their feet on the last kid's shoulders. When you're done, measure the room in grownups and compare the difference.

ANKLE DETECTOR

1-3

DO YOU HAVE A BLANKET, SHEET, BEDSPREAD, TABLECLOTH, AFGHAN, THROW, PONCHO, OR QUILT HANDY?

Have the kid lie down and cover them with a blanket. You are going to count to ten out loud. While you do, the kid can move around under the blanket to make it hard to find their ankles.

At ten, reach down and try to find an ankle. You get one point for each time you find an ankle. The kid gets a point each time you don't! Keep playing until you are laughing too hard to poke ankles. **Advanced level:** this time try to grab elbows!

LEANING TOWER OF PILLOWS

DO YOU HAVE ACCESS TO SOME PILLOWS, TEDDY BEARS, AND OTHER SOFT THINGS THAT YOU CAN STACK?

In this game you'll make squishy towers out of soft things that are bound to fall down.

Gather your soft building materials: pillows, stuffed animals, blankets, stuff like that. Now, work together to build a tower. What happens when you start with a big flat thing like a pillow, or a tall pointy thing like a stuffed rabbit? How high can you go before it falls down? WARNING: It is possible that a gentle pillow fight may ensue if the tower happens to fall on one or more players.

Now try and build one that's taller, or uses more things! You can work together to build a tower, or separately, and measure to see whose tower is the tallest.

FASHION FORWARD SCARECROWS

1+

DO YOU HAVE ACCESS TO A BUNCH OF CLOTHES?

This is a game about making scarecrows on the floor with loose, colour coordinated clothing.

Choose a colour and have everyone say it out loud together (start with blue for this first round). Kids work together to make a scarecrow on the floor using clothing of the named colour. Each scarecrow needs a top and a bottom, like a shirt and pants, or a dress and tights. Extra points for feet (socks), hands (gloves) and heads (hats). When you're done, name your scarecrow and take a picture next to it. Then choose a new colour. Keep playing until you've made enough scarecrows to keep the crows away forever.

Expert mode: see if the group can make a totally green scarecrow in under one minute. I don't see any crows around. Must have worked!

SILVER WHERE?

1+

DO YOU HAVE A BOOK, AND SOME SPOONS?

This is a game about placing pieces of silverware on a book without having them touch each other.

Lay a book flat on the table. This is your playing area. Place a piece of silverware anywhere on the book. Now the next player goes, putting the second piece on the book. The only rule is: it can't touch any of the other pieces! Keep taking turns adding more and more pieces of silverware. How long can you go without having any touch?

PILLOW PASS

3+

DO YOU HAVE A SOFA, AND SOME PILLOWS?

In this game everyone sits on a couch and passes along a pillow using only their legs and feet.

Sit all the kids close together on the couch and have them stick out their legs. Put a pillow on the first kid's legs. Without using their hands, the kids need to pass the pillow down the line. If the pillow makes it to the end, everybody wins! Start over if the pillow falls to the floor.

Pillow Points: see how many times the group can pass the pillow safely down the line. What about reversing the direction?

HIDE THE GROWNUP

1-3

DO YOU HAVE A FEW LARGE TOWELS OR SMALL BLANKETS AROUND?

This is a game where kids hide the grownup ... by tossing a towel over their head.

Give all the kids a towel and stand a few feet away from them. Now challenge the group to hide you under a towel. The only rule is: the kids can't move! Taking turns, have the kids toss towels onto your head. If they miss, try again. If they cover your head, everyone wins!

Tip: don't want a towel on your head? Have the kids toss towels at a stuffed animal instead.

SPOONER OR LATER

2-3

DO YOU HAVE A TOWEL OR NAPKIN, AND SOME SPOONS?

This is a game about finding hidden spoons.

Hide one spoon under the towel – crumple it up a bit to hide the spoon. Get everyone else to take turns putting one finger down on the towel. If you touch the spoon, you take it. Whoever has the most spoons after five games wins!

HOVERPAD RACE

1-3

DO YOU HAVE SOME TOWELS?

In this game the floor is lava and towels are safe hoverpads. Players hop from towel to towel to reach a goal.

Pick a starting line and a goal that's not too far away and give everyone a few towels. Have everyone 'design' their course by placing the towels between the starting line and the goal. When the race starts, players can only step on the towels. Start the race! How carefully can players reach the finish line? Remember, this is LAVA we're dealing with!

SOCK BOCCE

1-3

DO YOU HAVE FOUR ROLLED UP SOCKS PER PLAYER? AND ONE PAIR OF CLEAN UNDERPANTS?

Choose a throwing line and hand out four rolled up socks to each player. It is helpful if each player can remember which socks are theirs. Now, throw the underpants across the room!

Take turns rolling a sock towards the underpants. Try to get as close as you can. The person who gets a sock closest to the underpants wins! That means they get to throw the underpants across the room to start the next round.

ESCAPE FROM THE BURRITO

DO YOU HAVE SEVERAL SHEETS OR BLANKETS HANDY?

Get ready: the kids are about to turn you into a giant grownup burrito! Start by giving the kids a few blankets or sheets (the tortillas). Then stand in the middle of the room with your hands at your sides. You are now ready to be burrito'ed (gulp).

Begin the game: count down from twenty as the kids wrap you as tightly as they can in the sheets and blankets. When you reach zero, shake loose and chase the kids!

Tip: keep the sour cream away from the children.

THE QUIETEST MONSTER

(SNORING IS ENCOURAGED.)

Catch little monsters before they sneak out the door. Not the front door. An inside door!

Have everyone close their eyes and pretend to be asleep. Move to one side of the room and close your eyes. When you say 'Goodnight little monsters' everyone else can try to stand up and quietly sneak towards the door. If you hear someone moving, say 'Gotcha!' Anyone caught has to go back to their sleeping position. If someone sneaks out the door, they win!

Tip: try not to actually fall asleep when you play as a monster.

WHOSE SOCKS?

2+

DO YOU HAVE A SEVERAL CLEAN PAIRS OF SOCKS (BIG SOCKS ARE BEST)?

In this game players close their eyes and try to find (and put on) a matching pair of socks.

First, have all the kids sit in a circle. Put all the socks in the middle. Unroll them and mix them all up. Everyone has to close their eyes. Now each player has to grab two socks from the middle and put them on. NO PEEKING! Then, once everyone is wearing socks, have everyone open their eyes. Whoever has matching socks wins. And whoever has funny mixed up socks wins too!

DON'T SINK THE SHIP!

1+

DO YOU HAVE A SMALL PLASTIC CONTAINER AND A BUNCH OF HAND TOWELS?

Fill up the bathtub and float a plastic container on the water. The floating container is your ship. Give it a name (anything but The Titanic) and put it in the tub! If it doesn't float well, find a new ship that does.

Next, put your hand towels in a pile outside the tub. In a moment you're going to see how many the ship can hold without sinking! Taking turns, have each player take a towel, get it wet, and then gently place it on the boat. If the ship is still floating, do it again! Count each towel as you add it. How many can you get to before the ship sinks?

Competitive mode: play with an assortment of objects and try not to be the person who sinks the ship.

SYNCHRONIZED BRUSHING

1

IS IT TIME TO BRUSH YOUR TEETH?

Give the kid their toothbrush with a pea-sized amount of toothpaste. Grab a toothbrush for yourself, and stand facing the kid. In a moment, you will try to brush your teeth as if you were looking into a mirror – both of you brushing in the exact same way.

You'll start as the leader, and the kid will brush exactly the way you do... But when you wink, the kid becomes the leader and you copy them! Brush fast, slowly, in circles, up and down, and in different parts of your mouth. Wink again after a minute or two, and see if you and the child can spit at the exact same time!

BATHTUB SONAR

1+

DO YOU HAVE SOME DIFFERENT SIZED THINGS YOU CAN GET WET?

In this game the kids guess what something is by listening to it splash!

Fill the bathtub with water and find several things that can get wet. Show the objects to the kids and get them to say what each one is out loud. Now have them close their eyes, or turn away. They're about to try to identify each thing just by listening to it splash.

Start playing: pick something (but don't tell anyone what it is) and hold it high above the tub. Tell the kids to listen carefully, and then drop it. Can the kids guess what you've dropped, by listening to it splash? Keep playing until you've dropped all the objects, then find some more and play again!

BATHROOM BODY BUILDING

1

DO YOU HAVE A COMB OR HAIRBRUSH?

In this game the child lifts a comb up and down using only two fingers (good exercise for the finger muscles).

Find a comb (or a soft brush) and help the child balance it on their index and middle finger, while standing over the sink. Next, challenge the child to try and lift the comb over their head and down again, without the comb falling off. If they do it five times in a row they win! Cheer your support as they go: 'Ooh it looks heavy! Feel the burn! One more rep!'

Race mode: can the child do five finger-comb reps in under twenty seconds?

BUBBLE TROUBLE

1-2

DO YOU HAVE BUBBLE BATH? AND A COIN?

In this game, the kids try to find treasure hiding under the bubbles in the tub.

Fill up the tub and put in enough bubble bath to cover the surface with bubbles. Now drop in a coin! The kids in the tub have to find it by feeling around under the bubbles. Can they recover the treasure in three tries? Try adding more coins for more fun, just don't let them go down the drain! It's good clean fun.

GAMES FOR OUTDOORS

MAGIC CHARM

2+

DO YOU HAVE A SMALL OBJECT NEARBY, LIKE A COIN OR A PEN CAP?

In this game the kids lie down with their eyes closed and the grownup secretly hides something on one of them.

First, show the kids a small object. This is the magic charm. Explain that it will magically appear on somebody (it is very magical). Explain to the kids that in a moment they'll lie down and close their eyes – while you hide the magic charm in one of their pockets or socks (but not their ears).

Now start the game. While everyone is lying down, pretend to hide the charm in lots of different pockets and socks – tickle the players to distract them. At some point hide the charm, then keep pretending a bit longer. Confuse them! When you're ready, tell the players to stand up and find the magic charm. Whoever finds it gets to hide it next!

CATERPILLAR CRAWL

2+

ARE YOU A BUTTERFLY YET?

In this game, the group forms a caterpillar and races from the start to the finish line.

Choose a goal (not too far away) with some obstacles between you and it. Now get everyone into a conga line, one person behind another. You have just turned yourselves into a caterpillar! You are very fuzzy. To move as a caterpillar, the person in the very back of the line must run ahead and stand in the very front of the line. Practice moving like this a few times. Remember to chant 'Caterpillar! Caterpillar!' (that's what caterpillars say when they run). When you're ready, start racing! How fast can you 'caterpillar crawl' to the goal?

Challenge mode: mastered the caterpillar crawl? Split into teams and race.

MUD-BALL

2+

CAN YOU GET TEN OR MORE SOFT OBJECTS SUITABLE FOR ROLLING AND A PHONE?

In this game two teams compete to roll mudballs over to the other team's side. Choose a dividing line to split the playing area in half. Put half the players on one side, and the other half on the other. Evenly distribute the balls or objects to both sides.

The balls are mudballs – rotten, disgusting concoctions that will eventually explode goo! Tell everyone that when the game starts, players must STAY ON THEIR SIDE while rolling the icky mudballs over to their opponents' side. Get everyone set, then yell 'GO!' and start a timer on your phone. When the time runs out, whichever team has more balls on their side is covered in goo! Pretend goo. Unless you'd prefer to play with the real thing.

TEXT FROM A TREE

1+

IS THERE A SECOND GROWNUP WITH A PHONE WHO CAN HELP YOU PLAY?

In this game everyone tries to find the tree that's texting your phone. Ask the second grownup to take a picture of a nearby tree and text it to your phone with the caption 'Find me!' Tell everyone you're waiting for a message from a very important tree. When the text comes, show it to everyone and ask them to find the tree from the picture!

When the team finds it, pose for a new picture with the talking tree! Make the game harder by taking a close-up photo. Make it easier by including nearby landmarks in the photo.

FAIRY SHOWDOWN

1-2

DO YOU HAVE ROOM TO WALK THREE PACES?

In this game players walk three paces and then quickly shout out a rhyme, or else they'll turn into a pumpkin!

Players start back to back. Say 'ready, set, go!' and then players walk three paces away from each other. Count each step out loud. When you reach three, quickly turn around to face each other. Each player races to say any two words that rhyme with each other. The last player to make a rhyme is turned into a pumpkin! **Tip:** change the number of paces to suit the space you're in, or just to keep the fairies on their toes.

SLUG RACES

1+

THIS COULD TAKE A WHILE.

This is a simple race from the start to the finish line, except the goal is to come in LAST!

Line everyone up and pick something to be the finish line, but don't make it too far away. As slowly as possible, everybody creeps towards the goal. Players have to keep moving at all times, but they can go as slow as they want. Whoever gets there last, wins!

DON'T DROP THE WATERMELON

2+

DO YOU HAVE A BALL, OR SOMETHING SOFT YOU CAN TOSS?

In this game everybody works together to toss a 'watermelon' around without dropping it.

Gather the group in a circle and show everyone the ball. This is your watermelon. If you drop it, it will explode into a big sticky mess. As a group, race to pass the watermelon around the circle. See how fast you can go. If you make it all the way around, take a big step backwards and keep playing. You win if you can reach five steps back. But if you drop the watermelon, you have to start over again, and pretend to clean up the sticky mess! You could play this game with an actual watermelon, but we don't recommend it.

SUBMARINES!

1+

SPLOOOOOSH.

Start off by having all the kids crouch down on the ground. They're submarines. Now explain that you're the submarine commander!

When you point up, all the submarines need to slowly rise. When you point down, the subs need to slowly dive down.

To start playing (if you're in a place where you can make some noise), make a big submarine 'ayooooohag' sound, and then point up or down. Keep the submarines on their toes and switch directions often!

Admiral's advice: if you're in a place where you can be loud, shout 'DIVE! DIVE!' and 'SURFACE! SURFACE!' as you point.

FOLLOW THE MONSTER 2+

FOR MONSTERS, PEOPLE, AND PEOPLE PRETENDING TO BE MONSTERS.

Begin the game as the Big Monster and tell everyone else that they are Little Monsters. The Big Monster's job is to lead the Little Monsters over, under, around, through, between, next to, and on top of things around you. When the Big Monster moves, the Little Monsters follow behind in a line, copying the Big Monster exactly.

The Big Monster should tell the Little Monsters what they are doing as they do it. For example: 'The monsters are going UNDER the branch. Now the monsters are going OVER the rocks.' Play as the Big Monster until the Little Monsters get the hang of it. Then choose someone else to be the new Big Monster!

Tip: vary how the Big Monster moves. Frog-hop, run, and crawl over, under, and through things.

GLASSES VERSUS HATS 1+

ARE THERE A BUNCH OF PEOPLE AROUND, WHO WILL BE THERE FOR THE NEXT MINUTE OR TWO?

Ask each player whether they think more people are wearing hats or glasses. Then count the glasses wearers and hat wearers around you.

You can do this as a group, or assign one person to count glasses and another hats (people wearing both hats and glasses get counted in both categories). See whose original guess was the closest!

PEDESTRIAN PREDICTION 1+

STEP TO IT.

Pick something in the distance, but not too far away – like a tree, or that seat over there. Have everyone guess out loud how many steps they think it will take to get there. Make sure to guess in kid steps.

Now test your guess! Walk to the target and count each kid step. If anyone was exactly right, everybody do a dance! Now pick something new in the distance and play again.

DIZZY DASH

3+

ARE YOU PLAYING IN A PLACE WHERE THE GROUND IS SOFT ENOUGH TO FALL DOWN?

In this game the players spin around and then race to the grownup! Line up all the kids, while you stand 15 or 20 feet away. Shout out a number. The kids have to spin around that number of times, while everybody counts the spins out loud.

When everyone is done spinning, the kids run towards you. The first one to touch you gets to become the new finish line.

FINDER SEEKER

1+

ARE THERE LOTS OF DIFFERENT PEOPLE AROUND?

In this game kids look for people with a particular attribute.

Start by telling the players that they're all going to count the people wearing black shoes. With the kids, find people around you wearing black shoes and help them count each one. How many did the group count? Now try again, but this time count people wearing blue pants. Play again, but make up your own category.

THE MAGIC TOUCH

ARE YOU CLOSE TO SOMETHING?

In this game the kids will try and guess what they're touching – without using their eyes!

Set up the game: have the kid close their eyes and stick out their hand. In a moment you're going to place their hand on something around you. Begin the game: carefully guide the child toward an object (something like a tree, a fire hydrant, or a bush) and place their hand on it. Now see if the child can guess what they're touching. Give clues if they're stumped (even if they're stumped by a stump).

TURTLE, RABBIT, CHEETAH 1+

(OR MAYBE EVEN ROBOT.)

In this game the kids move like the animals that the grownup calls out.

First, explain to the kids that there are three special ways to move... When you say 'turtle' players should move slowly. When you say 'rabbit' players have to hop. And when you say 'cheetah' players run as fast as they can... At any time you can say 'kids!' and players have to walk like normal kids again. Start playing! Call out 'turtle', 'rabbit', or 'cheetah' from time to time as you walk.

Tip: you can always add more animals, or create new categories like 'robots'.

KNOCK IT OFF!

1-2

DO YOU HAVE SOMETHING SMALL AND SOFT THAT YOU CAN BALANCE ON YOUR HAND, LIKE A RUBBER BALL, A HAT, OR A LEMON?

You – the grownup – take something small and soft and balance it on the back of your hand. Have it balanced? Good. Now start the game: challenge the kids to knock it off using any (gentle) means necessary.

Encourage tickling, if you dare. Move around to avoid the kids' attempts. Remember, if the object falls off, YOU LOSE. Heh, heh, heh.

Grownup challenge: easy for you, hard for the kids? Don't raise your hand above the level of the kids' heads. Or try not moving your feet.

CHEESE SNEAKERS

3+

DO YOU HAVE THREE OBJECTS HANDY? THEY CAN BE ANYTHING KIDS CAN GRAB AND CARRY – SOCKS, BOOKS, TOYS, ETC.

This game is best played in a safe area, like the garden, or with the supervision of a second grownup. Kids will try to sneak up and take the cheese that a grownup is guarding without getting caught.

Line up the kids on one side of the space. They are the mice and they want to take your cheese! Sit on the ground and set three objects – the cheese – in a circle around you. You'll be guarding them, but with your eyes closed! Tell everyone that when you say 'GO', they can start crawling or walking around, trying to take the cheese. If you hear someone moving, try to reach out and grab them without opening your eyes or standing up. If a mouse takes a piece of cheese, they win! If you touch a mouse, they have to go back and start again. As soon as you're ready to play, close your eyes and shout 'GO!'

GUESS WHO'S AROUND YOU

ARE YOU IN A PLACE WITH LOTS OF OTHER PEOPLE AROUND?

Secretly choose a 'mystery person' around you, but don't say who! Now, have the kid ask you yes-or-no questions to figure out who it is. Do they wear glasses? Is it a girl? Are they playing bagpipes? When they think you know who it is, they can take a guess. Once they get it right, switch roles and play again.

RHYTHM MACHINE

3+

HAVE YOU GOT RHYTHM?

Start the beat! Use your feet to establish a regular pattern by stepping hard on the ground. Now have a kid join in and try to match your beat. Keep adding people to the beat. When everyone has it, change it a little bit and get everyone to join in the new rhythm. Keep it going as long as you can!

Challenge mode: have each kid lay down a different pattern. They can walk double-time, or drag one foot, or jump every fourth beat. Whatever they want, as long as they can do it over and over.

HORSESHOES WITH YOURSHOES

1+

ARE THE PLAYERS WEARING SHOES? AND ARE YOU IN A SAFE PLACE TO TOSS THEM A SHORT DISTANCE?

Place a target, like a hat or a magazine, on the floor. Now, have the players take off their shoes and stand 5 to 10 feet away. Players take turns tossing their shoes at the target. The player who gets nearest to the target is the winner! For a wilder version, try flinging the shoes with your feet instead of your hands.

Suggestion: make sure everyone gets their shoes back!

PICNIC YUCK-MIX

1+

WHAT AN UNPLEASANT PICNIC!

In this game, players imagine the yuckiest picnic ever. Start by saying 'I'm going on a picnic and I'm bringing a rusty old can!' The next player has to say 'I'm going on a picnic and I'm bringing a rusty old can and…' and then add something else grouchy.

Keep going – adding to the list each time – until you just can't remember anymore! Then say 'Uuuurgh!' and start again.

Bonus round: try playing the game alphabetically, starting with 'apple core'.

WALK THE TALK

PAY CLOSE ATTENTION.

In this game the kids have to watch and walk carefully.

You'll start off as the 'leader'. Choose a kid to start as the 'switcher'. The leader establishes the walk everyone walks – tiny steps, sideways, skipping, backwards – whatever they want. Start walking any silly way and have everyone copy you. At any point the switcher can call out 'switch!' When they do, the leader needs to immediately come up with a new type of walk. Everybody has to pay close attention to both the leader and the switcher! After a little while, choose a new leader and a new switcher.

STREETLIGHT, SIGNPOST, TREE

GET MOVING!

Secretly choose a clearly visible object a little way ahead (like a fire hydrant, a signpost, or a tree). Make sure it's a safe location. Don't say it aloud … yet! Tell the players to listen to what you are about to say: they have to run to the thing you tell them.

Build up with 'ready ... steady...', and then say the landmark you've chosen! The first person to reach it is the winner of that round. Name another landmark and keep going. Or if you prefer a less-competitive game, each player has to reach the landmark before you call out the next one. Try surprising the kids with a quick round of this game while you're on a long walk. It can help keep them moving.

MAGIC LINES 1-3

ARE THERE LINES AND CRACKS IN THE SIDEWALK OR GROUND WHERE YOU'RE WALKING?

Explain to the kids that for this game everyone can only walk on cracks and lines. If a player falls off, or needs to cross an open area, they must chant the Fairy Line-Rhyme, which goes like this: 'I'll be FINE when I get to a LINE!'

Begin! You should go first to demonstrate. Walk on cracks and lines, and then show players what happens when you have to cross an open space. Remember, the magic chant is 'I'll be FINE when I get to a LINE!'

PRETEND PARADE

3+

FORM A MARCHING BAND!

Line everyone up and give each marcher a role and accompanying movement. Choose someone to play the booming bass drum, someone to twirl the baton, and someone to play the trombone – marchers can make up their own assignments too!

Now start the parade! Everyone needs to march in time and do their movements. If they are so inspired, they can make the sound effects too. Lead the parade wherever you need to go, or wherever seems like the most fun! Extra points if passers-by stand and wave. Who needs floats?

DOGS AND SQUIRRELS

2+

ARE YOU IN A PLACE WITH SOME ANIMALS AROUND? DOGS ON WALKS COUNT.

In this game players make sounds whenever they see animals: when anyone sees a dog they say 'woof woof', and when anyone sees a squirrel they say 'awww nuts'!

There is one more rule: when you say 'switcheroo' players need to say 'woof' when they see a squirrel and 'awww nuts' when they see a dog. If there aren't many squirrels around, substitute birds and 'tweet tweet tweet' instead. Awww nuts!

APPENDIX

INDOOR GAMES

OUTDOOR GAMES

NUMBER OF PLAYERS	1	2	3	4+	PAGE
Caterpillar Crawl		●	●	●	27
Cheese Sneakers			●	●	37
Dizzy Dash			●	●	34
Dogs and Squirrels		●	●	●	44
Don't Drop the Watermelon		●	●	●	31
Fairy Showdown	●	●			30
Finder Seeker	●	●	●	●	34
Follow The Monster		●	●	●	32
Glasses Versus Hats	●	●	●	●	33
Guess Who's Around You	●				39
Horseshoes With Yourshoes	●	●	●	●	40
Knock It Off!	●	●			36
Magic Charm		●	●	●	26
Magic Lines	●	●	●		42
Mud-ball		●	●	●	27
Pedestrian Prediction	●	●	●	●	33
Picnic Yuck-mix	●	●	●	●	40
Pretend Parade			●	●	44
Rhythm Machine			●	●	39
Sluq Races	●	●	●		30
Streetlight, Signpost, Tree		●	●	●	41
Submarines!	●	●	●	●	31
Text From A Tree	●	●	●	●	28
The Magic Touch	●				35
Turtle, Rabbit, Cheetah	●	●	●	●	35
Walk the Talk		●	●	●	41

First published in Great Britain in 2016 by Osprey Publishing,
PO Box 883, Oxford, OX1 9PL, UK
PO Box 3985, New York, NY 10185-3985, USA
E-mail: info@ospreypublishing.com

Osprey Publishing, part of Bloomsbury Publishing Plc

A CIP catalogue record for this book is available from the British Library

Print ISBN: 978 1 4728 1597 2
PDF e-book ISBN: 9781472815989
EPUB e-book ISBN: 9781472815996

Printed in China through World Print Ltd

15 16 17 18 19   10 9 8 7 6 5 4 3 2 1

www.ospreygames.co.uk

Osprey Publishing supports the Woodland Trust, the UK's leading woodland
conservation charity. Between 2014 and 2018 our donations will be spent on
their Centenary Woods project in the UK.